THE PROFESSOR'S GROOVY POEMS

The Porfessor's Groovy Poems

ISBN: 978-0-9736308-7-9 (book)
ISBN: 978-0-9736-308-8-6 (hardcover)
ISBN: 978-0-9736308-9-3 (audio)

Welcome to the neighborhood, hep-cats.

I'm The Professor: your guide to all things poetry, people, and peculiar happenings. I'm tuned-in to all things beatsville and I can give you a tour if you'd like.

You'll see some real hip dudes and it's like, "Cool, man. She swings like a sixteen." You'll probably see some people you don't recognize- some off-the-wall cats- that seem a little funky. It's like, "Woah, man. That's way far-out," but don't sweat it. We're all cool.

The only rule to pick up on: sometimes life can be tough as toenails. So don't be square. Turn up the stereo; it's all groovy.

Groovy ave
1st

Be Careful With Your Belly

What's this on my belly?
I see you've got one too
Go ahead and poke it
And stick your finger through

Don't go in too far though
Your arm will disappear
Soon you'll have no shoulder
No neck, no chin, no ear

I do not want a friend of mine
To run around the place
With muscles on the outside
And bones instead of face

Be careful with your belly
If you poke and twist about
It's very, very likely
You'll end up inside out!

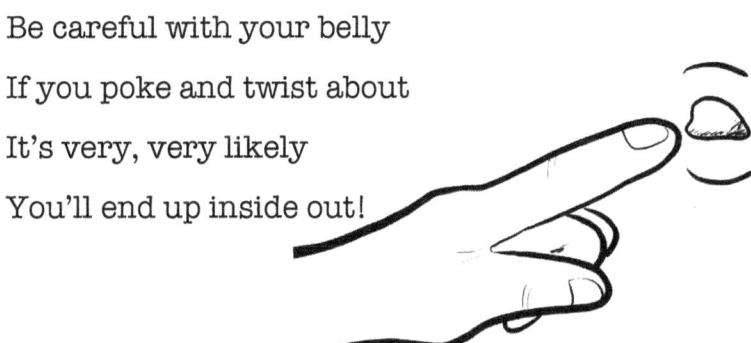

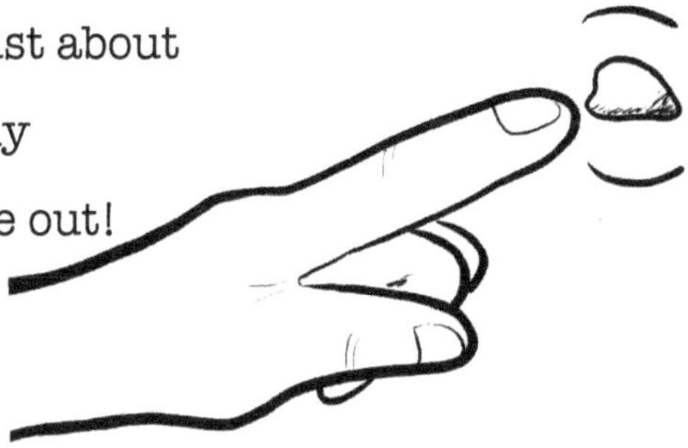

School Yard

I was listening in on the school yard discussions
Confused as a person can be
She said that she wants to have brown hair like he does
And they want some freckles like me

“I wish I had glasses like you over there”
“I want to have long feet and toes”
“I wish I had bouncy and curlied-up hair
How did you get it?
Nobody knows!”

“If only I had what he had every lunch”
And she wants the long legs that they have
They told me they stretched out their legs overnight
I don’t think they did...
They may have...

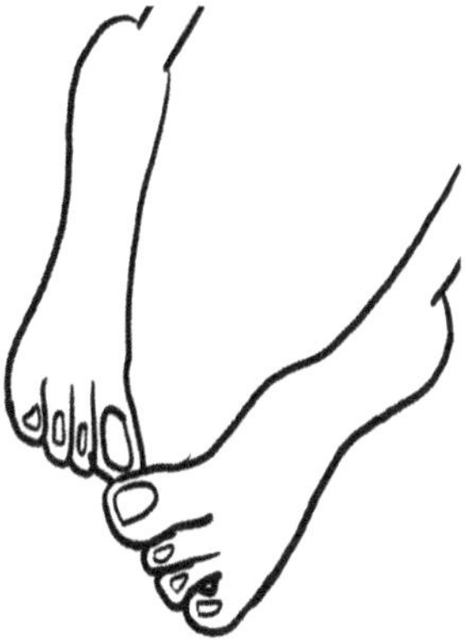

I think that I like my own hair after all
But her hat and his coat
I'd sure like to borrow
And maybe I'll stretch out my toes overnight
And see just how long they can get by tomorrow

Ooh Ah Ah Ah Ah!

I shouted down the bathtub drain
"Ooh ah ah ah ah!"

I shouted out the kitchen door
"Ooh ah ah ah ah!"

I shouted in the pouring rain
"Ooh ah ah ah ah!"

I shouted and I shouted more
"Ooh ah ah ah ah!"

I shouted from the mountain top
"Ooh ah ah ah ah!"

I shouted through my neighbor's mail
"Ooh ah ah ah ah!"

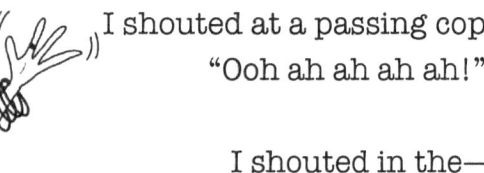

I shouted at a passing cop
"Ooh ah ah ah ah!"

I shouted in the—
Oh, I'm sorry . . .

You're not allowed to shout in jail

Book Report

I have to write a book report
The teacher said I must
I’ve read the book
Well, most of it
I want to but it’s just...

My thoughts are gone
I need a drink
Did I use disappearing ink?
My page is blank
What happens when
The words are clogged inside my pen?

I have to turn it in tomorrow
Do you have one that I can borrow?

Nosy Neighbor Nina

Nosy neighbor Nina is the nosiest of all
She often rests her nose atop our fence
To ask us where we're going and at what time we'll return
And other things intrusive and intense

"Well are you meeting others there?
And if so, when and whom?
I noticed that you're bringing chocolate cake
Is this perhaps a birthday
Or a wedding or a cook-out
A party or a fancy, new clam bake?

"Nina," I reply, "we're only meeting friends for dinner
Can't talk right now, you're going to make us late"
She asks with such disgrace, "Again?
I saw you doing dishes!
Be careful or you'll put on extra weight!

And furthermore, were you supposed to call the bank today?
I do believe your credit card is maxed
I called on your behalf and asked for January's statement
Debbie spent a fortune getting waxed!

And earlier today your creams and lotions were delivered
I signed for them and left them over there
It really is too bad that you and Debbie can't converse
I'm sure she give you all her extra hair"

But little does she know we aren't meeting friends for dinner
We're renovating and she's none the wiser

Tomorrow when she rests her nose
Upon our brand new fence
The current
Running through it
Will surprise her . . .

Go Quickly

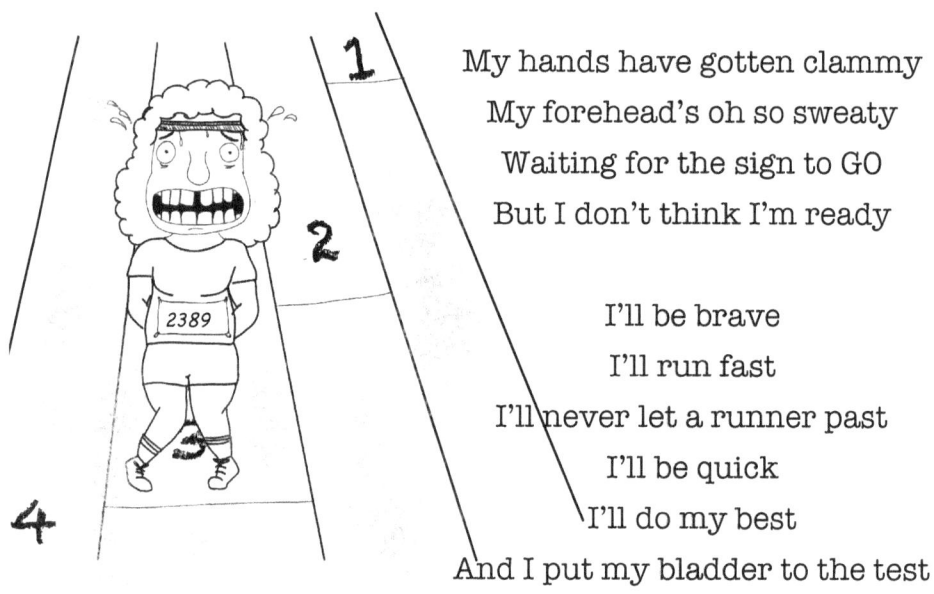

Lined up at the starting gate
My stomach's all aflutter
It's full of bouncing grasshoppers
My legs are slick like butter

My hands have gotten clammy
My forehead's oh so sweaty
Waiting for the sign to GO
But I don't think I'm ready

I'll be brave
I'll run fast
I'll never let a runner past
I'll be quick
I'll do my best
And I put my bladder to the test

You see
When I was getting ready
No one told this sweaty Betty
If you need the toilet, fine
But go before the starting line!

A E I O U and Why

I stubbed my big toe really hard
"Aaay-aaay-aaay-aaay-aaayyy!"

I snapped the waist of my leotard
"Eeee-eeee-eeee-eeee-eeeeee!"

I smacked my funny bone off the door
"Iiiy-iiiy-iiiy-iiiy-iiiyyyy!"

Then tripped and fell down on the floor
"Ohhh-ohhh-ohhh-ohhh-ooohhh!"

My toothbrush jabbed me in the cheek
"Yuuu-yuuu-yuuu-yuuu-yuuu!"

Wait . . . Do you always yell in vowels?

"Sometimes . . . Why?"

Ice Cream Order

Hello, good morning
Some ice cream today?
Eat it in-store or take it away
That sounds enticing, Can I ask a favor?
Tell me your best-selling favorite flavors

Chocolate, vanilla
And donutty dream
Salt water beaches
And peaches and cream
Walnutty moon-pie, and candied up yams
Strawberry flooty, and raspberry jams
Mocha-blast-chunkies
With white chocolate swirls
Cinnamon cheesy with jelly bean curls
Chocolatey flakies all dusted across
Twinkles and sprinkles
And caramel sauce
Whipped cream and dripped cream
Salami, bologna
A cookie on top in the shape of a pony
Coconut, apple, banana, and peach
What can I get for you?

One scoop of each

Tea Time

A fancy hat
Pinkies high
Would you like
Some crustless pie?

Tiny cups
Finest china
Nothing could be any fina

It's lovely having tea with you
Would you like one lump or two?

Beats prefer to take a short trip to Rio. Straight java, man.

Balloon Obsession

I'll take ALL of those balloons!!!

The red one

The yellow one

The blue one

The green one

The black one

I LOOOOVVE BALLOONS!!!

A purple one

A pink one

A rainbow one

Byyyyyyyyyyyyeeeeeeeeeeeeeeeeeeee!!!!!!

Nice to Meet You

Hello,
Nice to meet you
My name is Betty Netty
There's nothing I love more
Than eating big bowls of spaghetti

I'll introduce you to my friend
Their name is Putty Dutty
And they would love a serving of
Your sauciest spaghutty

Here's another chum of mine
His name is Rooty Tooty
His favorite thing for dinner
Is a big bowl of spaghooti

Have you met my lovely friend?
She goes by Patty Natty
And when she's out for lunch
She orders two plates of spaghatti

And this Ted
His mother said
"He's plain as Jane
From toe to head
He'll never eat spaghetti, instead
A single piece of Wonder Bread"

Lunch Games

I want you to know
That I will be thinking
And laughing at lunch time today

I left you a game
A riddle of sorts
A fun little something to play

A day that is filled up with work is so boring
No falling asleep, no dozing or snoring
But when it comes lunch time the games will begin
A hide-and-seek sandwich for lunch
Dig in!

It's not in the fridge and it's not at the store
You'd best take this shovel though
That is for sure!

I hope that you wrapped it
In paper or plastic
Or else, I would hope that
The dirt tastes fantastic!

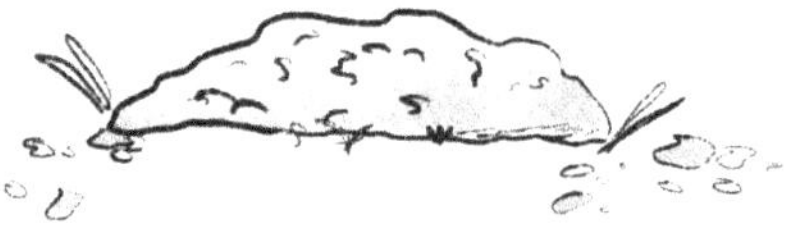

Body Parts

What happens if my parts
Decide to grow at different times?

One foot big
The other small
One side short
The other tall
One arm stretched
The other little
Belly button
Not in the middle

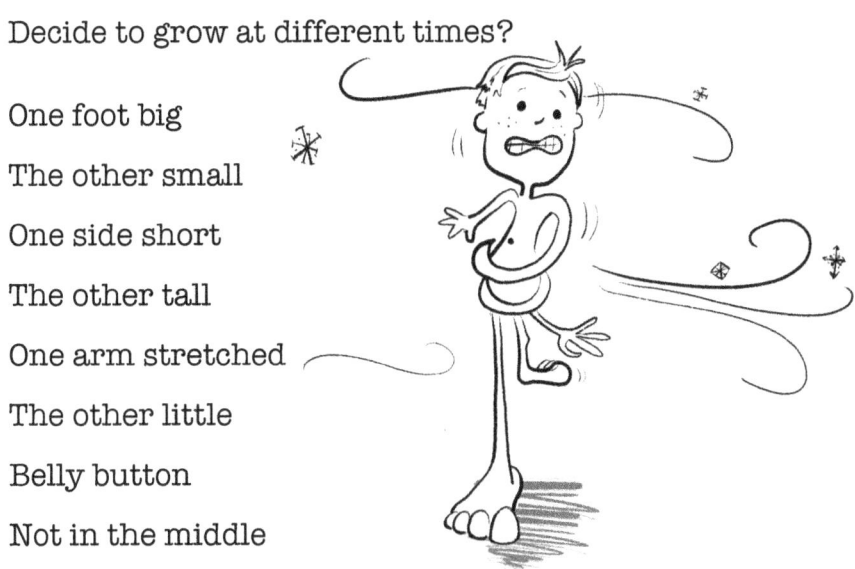

Riddle me this: is this where I'm going?
Tell me it's not how I'm gonna be growing!

"Just eat your veggies and you'll be okay
You'll grow up and then you'll be taller someday."

But nevertheless
How will I know
That each of my parts
Will know when to grow?
My clothes will not fit if I grow willy-nilly
And I will be naked!
And that will be chilly...

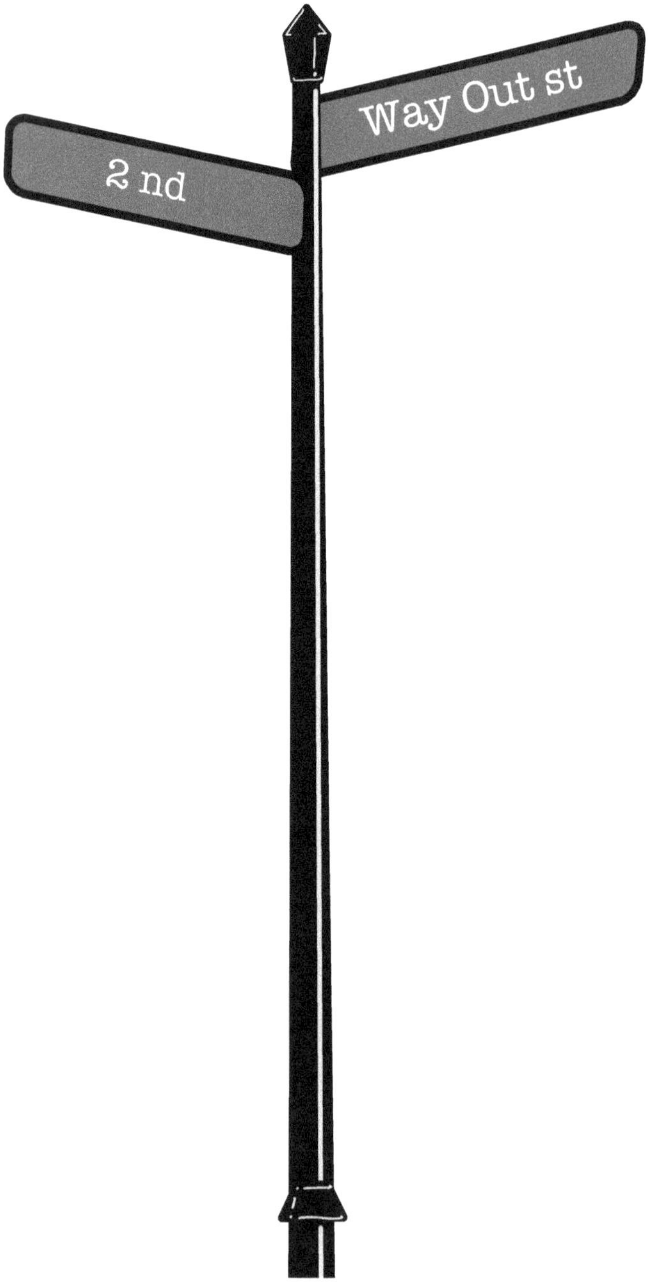

2 nd
Way Out st

The Best Pet Ever!

I think I'll get a pet!
I want someone to love

A colorful parrot
He'll be my best friend
I'll share all my secrets . . .
Nah
Too talky

An elephant would be fun!
Flappy ears, wrinkly skin, great big feet. . .
Nope
Too stompy

A giraffe would be perfect!
With knobby knees and neck sooo long
She'll sleep in the . . .
Ugh!
Too stretchy

Oooh! A cheetah!
Super fast and great at games
No, wait
Too cheaty

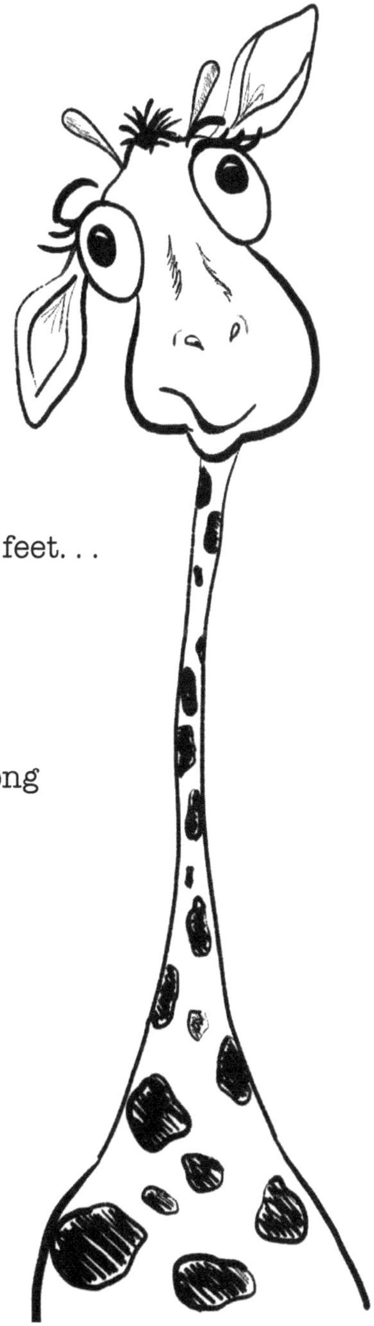

A fancy porcupine
Oh, sooo fine!
We could cuddle all night . . . NO!!
Too pokey

A dragon would be great!
Oh, the places I could fly
With breath like flames . . .
Hmmm
Too fiery

A chameleon would be awesome
We could play hide 'n seek . . .
Oh, shoot
Where'd he go???

A worm would be nice
We could go fishing on the weekends. . .
Um... nope

A teeny tiny tsetse fly!
Nice and tsetse
But ICK!

A rock
A rock could be just right
A lovely rock
Smooth and quiet
Solid
My brand new pet!

Penelope Perdue

Cheeky and sassy are words that describe
Penelope Penny Perdue
She speaks in tongues and yields to none
Even when just passing through

Clearly she's needing a lesson or two
In manners and how to be kind
She slurped on some melon and spat out the seeds
And hit my behind with the rind

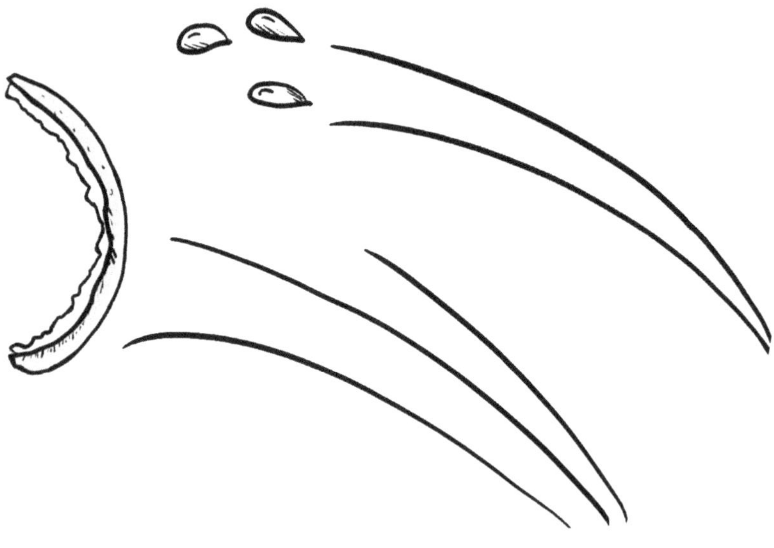

She's nasty to all and quick to dismiss
A friend or a stranger, a Mister, a Miss
We all stay away whenever she's near
The day that she leaves we'll erupt into cheer

But one blessed day our prayers were heard
Penelope left without saying a word
With her head in the clouds and her nose pointed high
She mustn't have heard all the neighborhood cry

"Watch out Miss Perdue!"
She hardly did wince
She fell in a hole
We've not seen her since

Here I Sits

Here I sit with just my thoughts
Scrambled up in bunched-up knots
That little voice inside my head
Has taken off and gone to bed

The one that's good at making sense
I think it jumped the backyard fence
It must have seen me counting sheep
When I was s'posed to be asleep

I wonder when it's coming back
Or if it's hit the road, Jack
Cause if it's gone for many years
I'll just have space between my ears

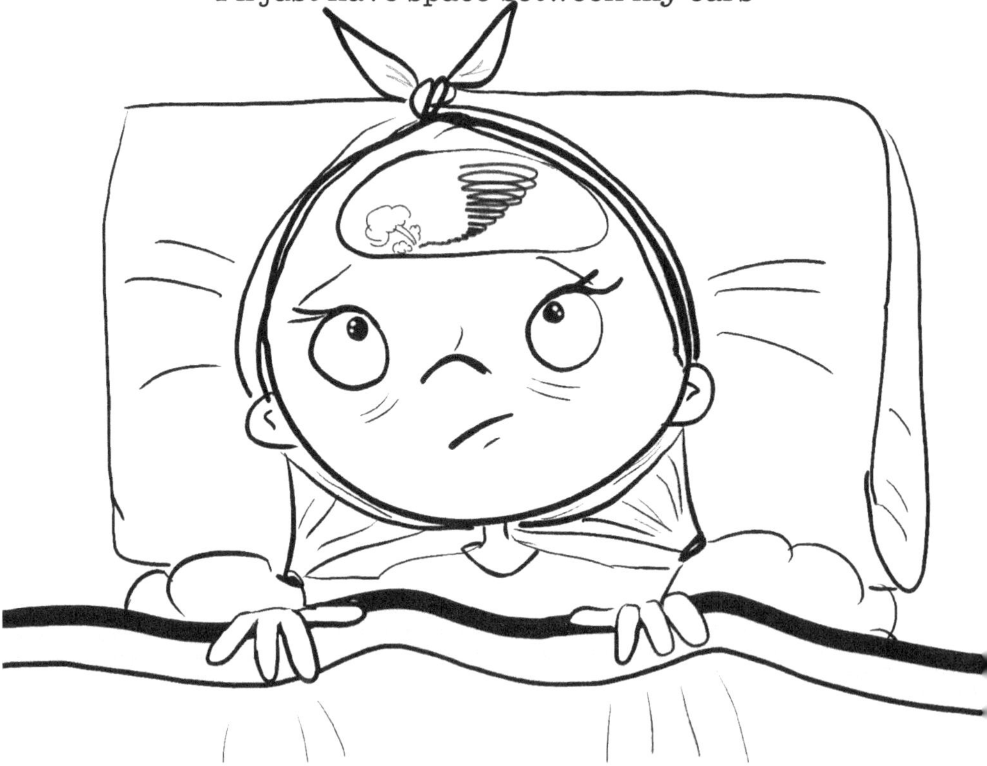

Quiet in the Library!

SHHHHHH!
You're in the library
The grumpy lady scorned
You MUST be quiet
Please DON'T speak
Now you've all been warned

Don't bend the pages, shelve the books
Or rip the old dust jacket
The spine should always stay in tact
Don't bend it back and crack it

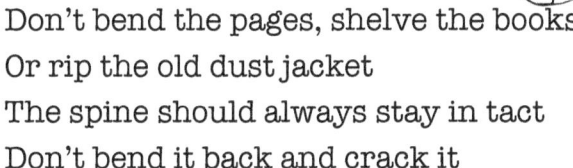

She slid her glasses down her nose
To see I'd make no noise
I'll do my best to be a mouse
And walk about with poise

My top half got the message
That's a guarantee
Although I've just had beans for lunch
I guess we'll wait and see

Francis Yoo

Francis Yoo was Forty-two
And knew no words but, "Doobie-Doo"
Oh, Francis Yoo, how do you do
The things you do at forty-two?

Dear Francis Yoo, what do you do
When ordering your morning brew
If you are asked, "One cream or two?"
Must you respond with, "Doobie-Doo"?

Francis Yoo you make me blue
I do not wish to speak to you
Because I haven't any clue
What could you mean by, "Doobie-Doo"

And if the things you say are true
You know no words except the two
I pray for your poor friends, I do
Whatever shall they Doobie-Doo . . .

My Friend

Today I was bored so I painted a friend
His mom got real mad so I washed him
But then!
She left us alone so I'll paint him again

Burps and Slurps

I drank a lot of soda
About 100 slurps
And now
There's bubbles in the tub
My bottom's got the burps

Camping Trip

Blow up bed
Lamp for head
Sleeping bag and book unread
Sticks for meats
Gooey treats
Drums to play some slappin' beats

Spray for bugs
With buzzing wings
And creepy, crawly, yucky things
Can of beans
Big canoes
Can't forget my rubber shoes

Pop up tent
Lots of poles
Something good for digging holes
Walking stick
Match for fire
I am losing my desire
Ear-flap hat
Welcome mat
Big backpack to hold all that. . .

All the places I can roam
Wait . . .
There is no room for my toothbrush . . .
I guess I'm staying home

creepy camping tales
WELCOME
BEANS
Spray

The Garden Gnome

Have you seen my garden gnome?
He always stands right there
Amongst the tulips, ferns, and trees
The wind a blowin' through his hair

Now a pile of tiny clothing
Sits where he should be
Some pants, a shirt, a pair of socks . . .
A gnomey mystery

FLASH!!!

Did you see that flash of skin?
It dashed into the bush
A hat, a beard, a big ol' gnose
A teeny-tiny tush

I guess he must've gotten bored
Standing still all day
He sought a little freedom
So he up and streaked away!

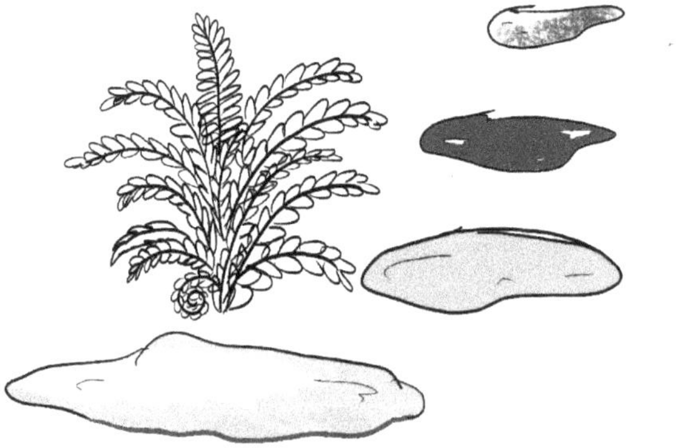

Farrah Fortune Teller

Farrah Fortune teller rolled her fortune telling cart
Down the road, around the bend
And parked at Millie's Mart

She drew the drapes and rummaged
For her favorite voo-doo doll
She lay out 50 Tarot cards and one big crystal ball

She lit some candles, poured her potions into little vials
And set out every tchotchke
That she'd carted miles and miles

But after seven days she hadn't seen a single face
And feared that she would soon become
A phony and disgrace

In order for Miss Farrah to attract a bigger crowd
She lit up her marquee
'Cause it was bright and it was loud

She plugged it in and, boy, it shone
For 15 seconds flat
But soon her cart began to spark,
Ignite, and that was that

Detectives figured,
"Her marquee was what had blown the fuse"
Too bad she couldn't fortune tell
The proper bulbs to use

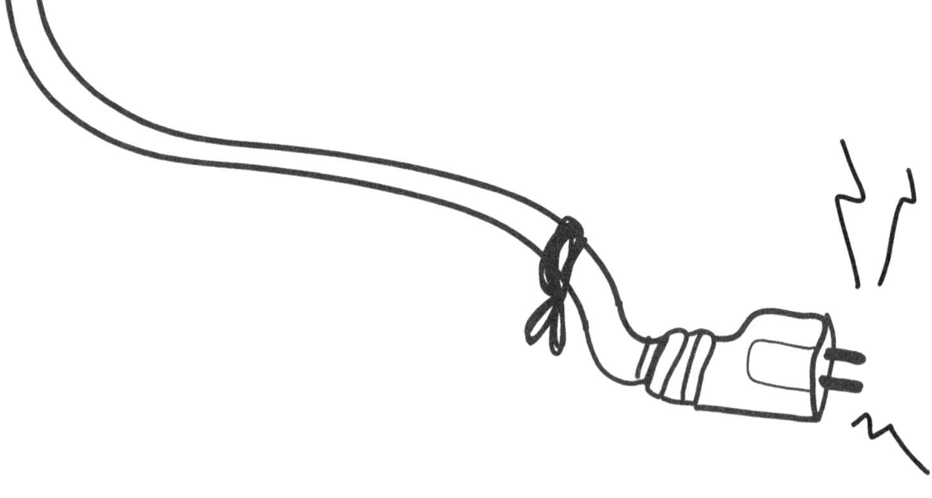

Talk about blasting the Edison!

You-ness

“Well, Doctor, it all started when I asked my mother . . .”

"How do I make people like me?
How do I keep them around?
How do I get them to think that I’m clever?
How do I make them remember my name?

What if they think I’m a weirdo?
What do I say to them then?
What if they tell me I’m wasting their time?
What if they think all my stories are lame?"

She told me, “My dear, the one thing you have
That nobody else ever did:
A clearly remarkable thing they call “you-ness”
No “you-ness” and you’re just some boring old kid

People will cheer when they see you have “you-ness”
“You-ness” will keep everybody around
“You-ness” is clever in every way
People remember when “you-ness” was there

Nobody ever thinks “you-ness” is weird
“You-ness” would never waste anyone’s time
“You-ness” makes everyone’s day so much brighter
When people see “you-ness” they listen
They care"

Turns out she didn't mean
My own uniqueness
My smartness
My boldness
My new-ness
Turns out she meant
Take my cousin along
The family favorite: Eunice

The Big Sneeze

Look at all these teeth!
Who belongs to these?
A set of teeth just lying there
Let me ask you, please

Holy ew!
What's that you say?
It happens almost every day?
With every big ol' Grandpa sneeze?

Call off the tooth fairy
He's still using these

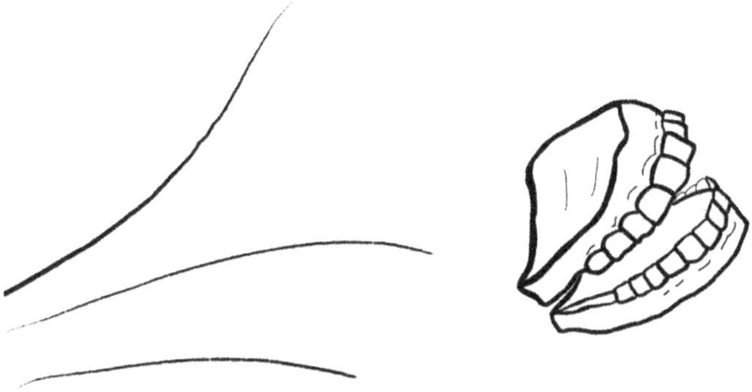

My Thoughts

My thoughts are like a forest
They grow out of my head
Some thoughts are big
Some thoughts are small
And some thoughts make no sense at all

Sometimes they help me know the things
I don't already know
Sometimes they're just plain silly
When I follow where they go

They take me on adventures
They're filled with pure delight
The only problem is
Sometimes...
They keep me up all night

Pesky Mosquito

Pesky lil' mosquito
Buzzin' in my ear
Can't you see I'm tryin'a sleep?
Go on, Get outta' here!

BBBBZZZZZZZZZZZZZZZZZZZZZZZZZ

Swat! Clap! Whoosh! Smack!
A-ha! I think I got 'em!
Oooouuch!
You win, you dreadful thing
You've bit me on my bottom!

Drip Splat Sploosh

Drip...

Drip...

Drip...

Drip...

Drip...

Drip...

Drop

The rain is coming down on me

Drip, splat, sploosh

It makes me cold and wet, you see
Drip, splat, sploosh

My boot has got a hole in it
Swish, splash, slosh

My toes are wrinkling up a bit
Swish, splash, slosh

The puddle is inside my boot
Slop, splash, splosh

My sock is wet and squishy . . . shoot!!
Squish, squash, skwoosh

Now I'm soaking wet
From my head down to my feet

But I'mma keep on walkin'
To this funky, squishy beat!

Drip drop splat sploosh
Squish squash sqwat skwoosh

Slip slop floop flop
Splish splash shloop shlop

Jazzy

Portals, The

...Through the portals
Julie jumped
She knees her scraped and head her bumped
And learned the quickly portal world
Had turned her downside out

She tried to words the find to say
How did here get she anyway?
The passing help she'd ask for man
He'd out with know a doubt

"Exsir me scuse," asked Julie now
"Exactly here I've gotten how?"

He looked her down and up and said
"This world is not for mortals

Go left ahead and take a straight
Unlock the fence or hop the gate
And all that's left for you to do is
hop back. . . .

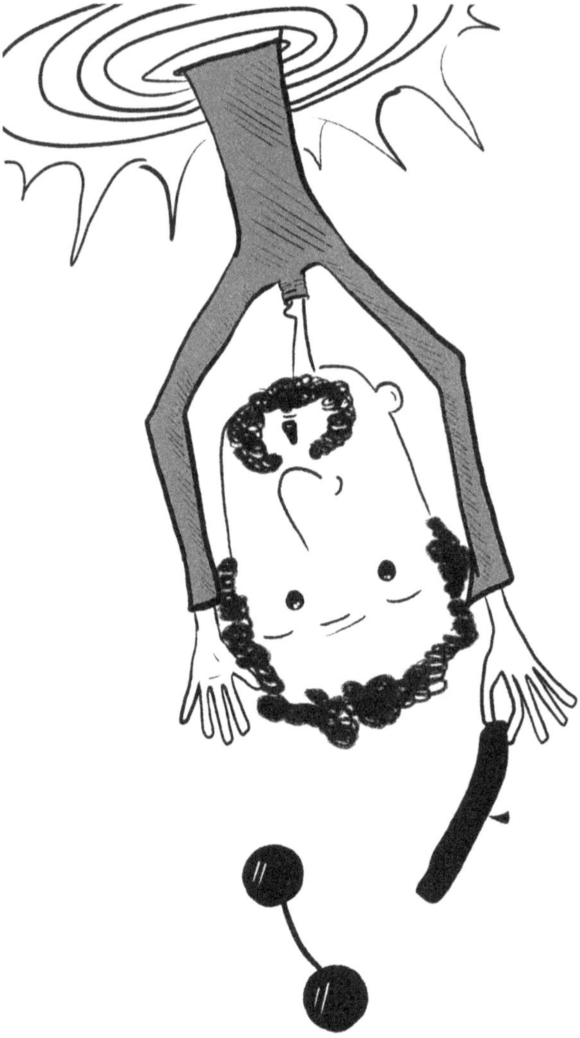

Far out!

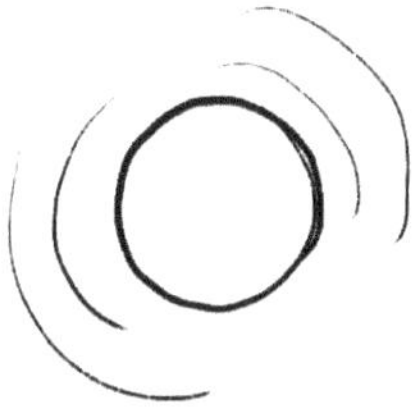

Frosty Yipths

Wanna know
The greatest snack?

A frozen popsicle!

A frosty treat to beat the heat
Cools you off from head to feet

Hold the stick

Take a lick

GAHH!!

Ith thtuck to my yipths!

You Forgot Your Face

Last night the winds blew warm
Something strange took place
My snowman slid
Straight outta' town
And forgot to take his face!

Swingin' st
3 rd

Shoping List

Can of peas
Batteries
Watermelons
Seven, please!
Jar of jam
Slice of ham
Forty dollars?
What a scam!

Pomegranate
Juice it
Can it
All the shampoo on the planet
Pans
Pots
Polka-dots
Yards of twine that's tied in knots

Extra socks
Keys and locks
Teeny-tiny pocket clocks
Paper towel
Wooden dowel
Bird cage for my neighbor's owl

Laundry soap
Braided rope
Add a giant cantaloupe
Oaty-o's
Baby clothes
Tissue for my runny nose

Tortellinis
Two bikinis
Extra beefy hotdog weenies
Lettuce head
Loaf of bread
Pillow cases for by bed

Purple beets
Shoes for feets
Condiments and deli meats
Fancy crown
Ballroom gown

Are you writing all this down?

Coffee beans
Collard greens
Size-eleven denim jeans
Dozen eggs
Soap for legs
Pokers
Pinchers
Pins and pegs

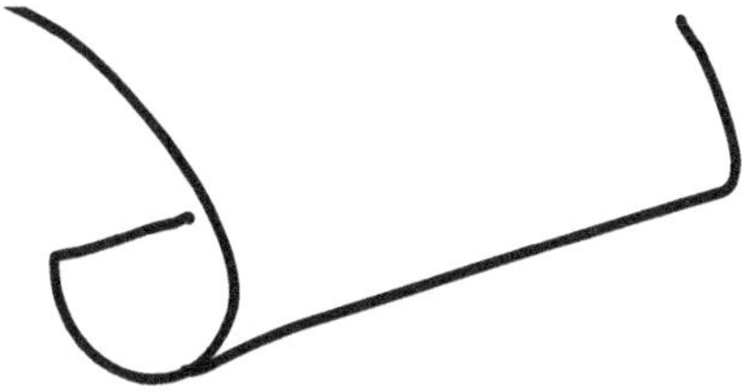

Swishy skirt
Satin shirt
Muddy mulchy bag of dirt
Avocado
Eldorado
Do re me fa sol ti la do

Alphabet soup
Bottle of goop
Extra-extendable basketball hoop
Pockets for pants
Jazzy new dance
Super high heels that will heighten my stance

Razors for shaving
Headlamps for caving
Think of the millions of dollars we're saving
Hiding the items inside of your beard
Just walk out quickly and don't make it weird!

PHHTTT!!!

I wish that I could whithle
I can't do it anymore
'Cause thinth I lotht my two front teeth
I thpit upon the floor

The Wonder of a Wonder

The Dreadful Squeak

Jeremiah Bleak
Too afraid to speak
For he couldn't figure out
What made that awful, dreadful squeak

In his head, he feared it
Each time he went heared it
Squeeeeeeak . . .
There it was . . .
Squeeeeeeak . . .
And again . . .

He scrunched down in bed
Riddled with dread
Was he making it up?
Was it all in his head?
Who was squeaking the squeaky, old door?
Squeeeeeeak . . .

Who was squeaking the creak in the floor?
Squeeeeeeak . . .
Squeeeeeeak . . .

A rubber shoe?
Oh, what do to?
Maybe a mouse?
Quick, Jeremiah!
Run from the house!

Straight out of town
With your bones a clinking
Before you get eaten
No time for thinking!

Pinchin'

I'm waiting in line for the coaster
Wearing my brandest new shoes
I'm waiting till everyone sees how they—

Uh oh
My shoes are pinchin'

My shoes are pinchin'
Oh, brother
Maybe I can hop on one foot
Then the other

Now my knees are knockin'
Oh, dear
Maybe I can bend one this way
And one here?

Now my arms are achin'
Oh, ouch
Maybe I can walk bent over
In a crouch

Now my spine is twistin'
Oh, my back
I don't think I'm fixin' this one
It's outta whack

I asked this gal,
"Excuse me, ma'am
A helping hand or two?"

She turned and looked
Said, "Holy COW!
What the heck are you!?"

You heard me say
I'm pinchin'
I'm knockin'
I'm achin'
I'm twistin'

My body is twizzlin'
Oh, heck
You heard me complain'
What did you expec?

Somebody get a doctor on the horn.

The Hug

I wanted to give you a gift
But I haven't got money to spend
I'll give you a gift from the heart instead
On this, you can always depend

It's a snuggly hug
A big bear-wuggly hug
A squishy-swishy
Goldfish kissy
Giant kinda' huggly-hug

A fuzzy-wuzzy
Giggly-wiggly
Plumpy-lumpy
Squeezy-weezy hug!

And if you think that this will do
I will take one back from you

Worst Day EVER!

I called my teacher, "Mom"
I called my teacher, "MOM!"
I feel like a dope
There isn't much hope
I called my teacher, "Mom"

I burped out loud in math
I BURPED out loud in math
My belly wiggled
People giggled
I burped out loud in math

I dozed right off in class
I DOZED RIGHT OFF IN CLASS
A big 'ol snort
The sleepy sort
I dozed right off in class

I farted in the gym
I FARTED in the gym
In the rainbow parachute
A teeny, tiny, tooty toot. . .
I farted in the gym

This is the worst day ever at school!

I feel like a looney

I feel like a fool

I wish I could simply

Just lay down and cry

Wait . . .

Did you say it's recess?

K Byyyyeee!

So Many Socks

Knitted ones, fitted ones
Comfy when I'm sitted ones
Bunchy ones, scrunchy ones
Good for eating lunchy ones

Mismatched, full of holes
Grippy on the slippy soles
Ones with toes, fancy bows
Stretchy-out for when I grows

Full of spots and polka dots
Look at all the socks I've gots!!!

My lucky feets get one sock each
Except for when I'm at the beach

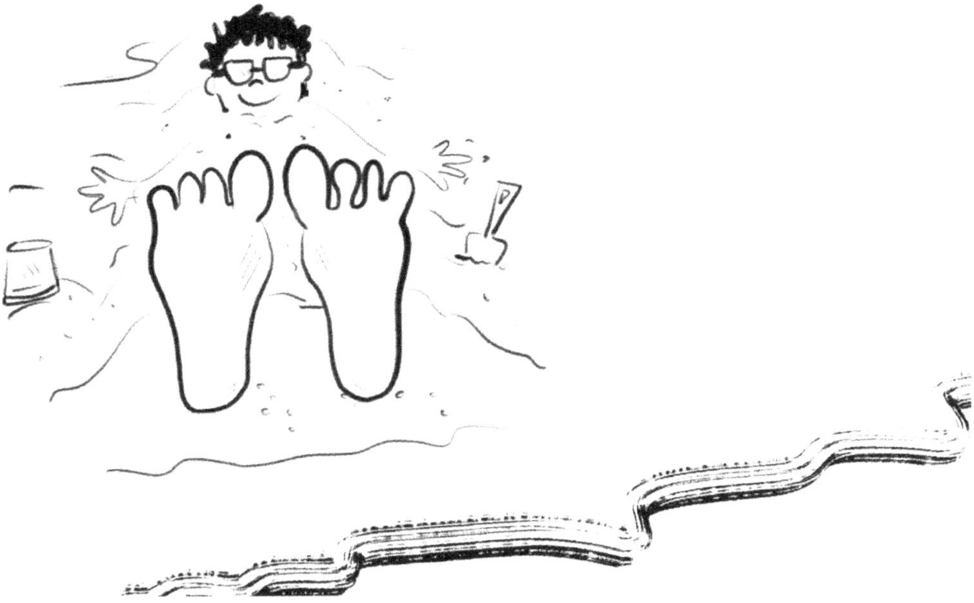

Sir Lance Les Pants

Here we have Sir Lance Les Pants
The Pants Prince
From the South of France
Whose pants would fall with every dance
How sad for good Sir Lance Les Pants

"To Court of Queen Suspender, now
Les Pants will not surrender now!"
The Queen refused to lend her
Son one measly old suspender

"How then," asked Sir Lance Les Pants
"Am I supposed to spin and dance
Or run and jump and twirl and prance
If 'round my ankles sit my pants?"

"We'll off to good King Belt and Buckle
Beg him, and with any luck he'll
Help us and we all will chuckle
Charge to Kingdom Belt and Buckle!"

"I'm sorry, sir
The king has died"
King Belt and Buckle's guard replied
Sir Pants turned 'round
He shrugged and sighed
"We have no use
He's gone and died"

In his court Sir Pants did hope
He wouldn't always look a dope
For now though, he could only mope
And sit so very still and hope

Until the garment shop in town
Presented him a brand new gown
No longer would he be a clown
And now he's known as Lance Les Gown!

Wailin' blvd
4 th

Toest and Jam

What is this between my toes?
It's fluffy and it smells

What's that you say?

It's jam, you say??

Then on my toast if goes!

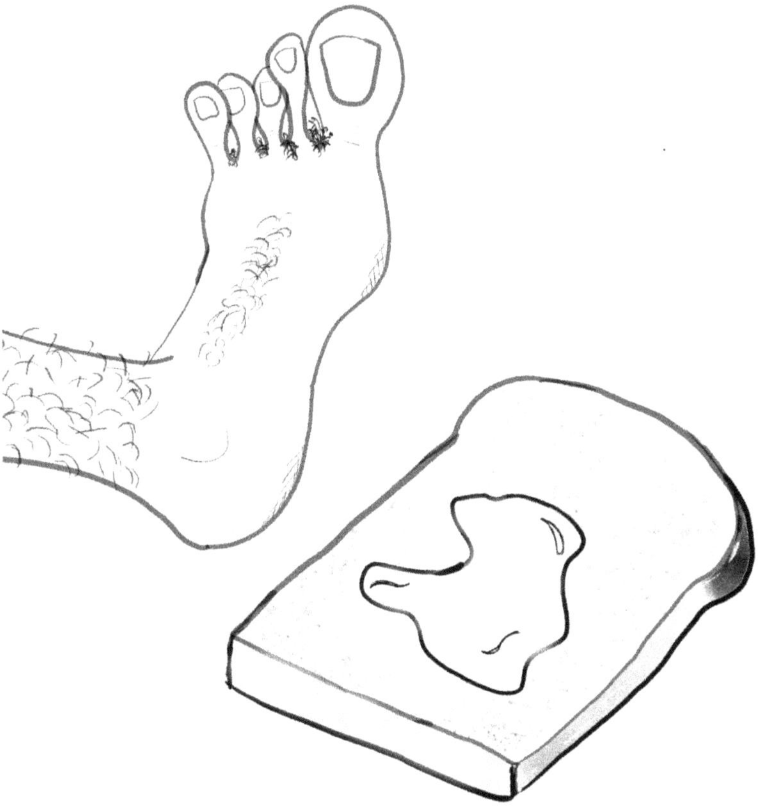

Tire Swing

My dearest, oldest tire swing
You giant rolly, rubber ring
It's been so long since I got on
But, oh the joy you always bring!

I surely missed the breezy breeze
The pollen makes me wheezy sneeze
But I will sneeze into the breeze
Just one request
No spinning, please!
The twirling makes me nauseated
Then it makes me sick
If you could stop the spinning
Please!

Then that would do the trick

I guess you didn't hear me then
My knees are getting weak
My stomach's churning, turning knots
My words I can't quite speak

Off, now I am getting

I take it can't no more

Find the bathroom now

But I...

I can't get off the floor!

Ruthy B. Ramone

Ruthy B. Ramone played a big ol' brass trombone
Every night from dusk 'til half-past five
When Ruthy B. Ramone started wailin' on trombone
The neighborhood would spark and come alive

Layin' 'neath the moon
She busted out a tune
As all the neighbors poured into the streets
They were dancin' they were singin'
Everybody's hips a-swingin'
To the rhythm of Miss Ruthy's rooftop beats

But little did she know that seven floors below
Was nasty, crusty, dusty ol' Philipe
The music made him rage
"THE ROOF IS NOT A STAGE!
THE STREETS ARE NOT FOR SAMBA!
LET ME SLEEP!"

His ears were plugged with plugs
He'd taken sleeping drugs
And he'd cranked his air conditioner up to ten
When suddenly he heard
Not a note and not a word
That is, until they started up again. . . .

"I do not understand!
We do not need a midnight band
I tell you, if this riot doesn't cease
I'm left without a choice
Nonetheless I will rejoice
When this party's broken up by the police!"

At twenty-five past two, strolled in Miss and Mrs Chu
Who looked around but didn't see a riot
Just Ruthy B. Ramone with her big ol' brass trombone
They asked her nicely, "Please just keep it quiet."

The dancers danced their feet
Into their homes and off the street
Donned their PJs and their nighttime facial creams
And Ruthy B. Ramone finally packed up her trombone
Brushed her teeth and dreamed some jazzy dreams

When downstairs, ol' Philipe
Didn't hear a single peep
Not a tap shoe, no parade, nothing at all

But with Ruthy out of sight
He heard his neighbor every night
And his wheezy, breezy, sneezy, snootin'
Rootin-tootin', air-pollutin'
Grumbly, rumbly snoring through the wall

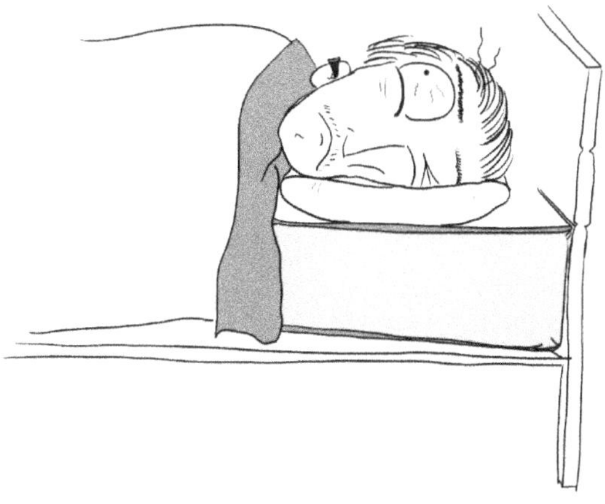

Wail away, Miss Ruthie!

Who Do I Look Like?

You look just like your father
Ooh ahh
If your father shaved his beard
Ooh ahh

You look just like your mother
Hmm ohh
If your mother's face was weird
Hmm ohh

You could look like your brother
Yes, sir
If he had a creepy stare
Yes, sir

Or even like your sister
Yes, ma'am
If she never washed her hair
Yes, ma'am

I'll trim a little off the top
Snip, snap
And a tiny bit more
Snip, snap

And suddenly you look . . .
Oh my!
Like no one's looked before!

Sensible Balloon

Pop!

Pop!

Pop!

Pop!

Pop!

One balloon is nice

Pop!

Pop!

Pop!

Pop!

Just one green balloon please

The Barbaras

I'm starting to feel really gross. . .
I think the Barbaras are coming
My stomach is suddenly aching. . .
I think the Barbaras are in town
I'm tossing and turing at night
I think the Barbaras are coming to visit
I'm feeling like –
KNOCK, KNOCK!!
The Barbaras are here. . .
Who is it. . . ?

They break down the door
With incredible force
Tossing out lies
Without any remorse
Too busy, too stupid
Too ugly, too tired
Not funny, no friends, no time
You've expired
Big disappointment, an awful disgrace
A horrible, terrible, lumpy, old face

“Just try to stop us– bet that you can’t!”
The horrible Barbaras continue to chant
I take a deep breath and say

“LISTEN UP, YOU BARBARAS!”

Sort yourselves out, I’m taking a walk
Figure it out and then we can talk
You weren’t invited
You’re hanging around
And making a horrible, terrible sound!

“I want a glass of water,” I hear a Barbara say
“I want to move around. I’ve been inside all day”
“I want to eat a vegetable or something green for lunch”
“Straighten up my posture! Look, my back is in a hunch!”

“LISTEN, BARBARAS, LISTEN!

Just get it when you need it
Then let me work and let me sleep
And goodness gracious
BEAT IT!!!”

My Pencil

I want to draw a picture
But my pencil will not play
My head, it shows me many things
That don't turn out that way

My pencil's really stubborn
It won't draw what I see
A bird, a tree, a robot
Please!
It's awful as can be

Fine I say, "You have a turn
Let's see what you can do"
And just like magic
Holy cow!
Something new began to brew

It started off unclear as day
With nothing making sense to me
But as I let my pencil draw
It got as clear as clear could be

At first it looked like squiggle-oos
Scribbley, squirrelly, swirly-os
I closed my eyes
And let my pencil
Draw its twisty, twirly-os

My everything felt happy
As my heart came out to play
My pencil flowed around the page
And had its swoopy, loopy way

So now I understand it all
I missed the missing part
My pencil isn't stubborn
No!
Sometimes my pencil draws by heart

My Bicycle

I’m saving for a bicycle
A big Banana Seat
Chopper bars and side view mirrors
Coolest on the street

A jazzy, swayin’ basket
And bell to go, “‘Briiing briiiing!”
So as you hear me coming through
Your heads will turn and swing

“Ooooh! Sick”
The people say
“Can I get one just like that?”
“What a ride!”
The people shout
You're one snazzy wheelin'-cat!”

I close my eyes and feel the breeze a-blowing in my hair
Cruising all around the town without a single care

I'm saving every penny, man
And won't it be so sweet
But for now
If I want to cruise...
I'll have to take my feet

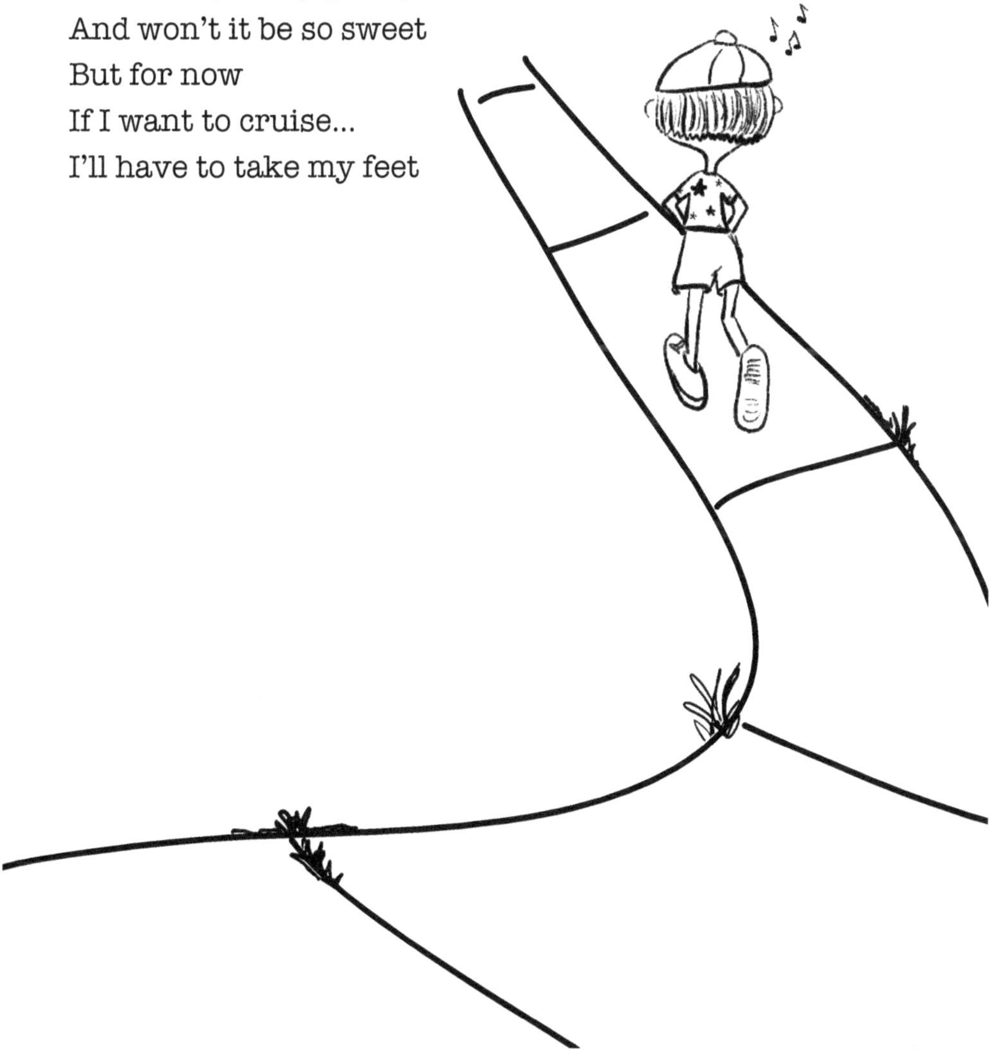

The Twistaloos

Bernice Twistaloo
Has joints that bend in two
She's flexy from her toes up to her crown

Contorted, twisted form
She doesn't know the norm
And no one ever knows her up from down

How is she doing that thing she does?
How is she bending in half?
How is she touching her head to her heels
And her neck to the back of her calf?

With rubbery bones from her mother
With noodly arms from her dad
The stretchiest neck on her brother
The Twistaloos all have gone mad!

They are rolling out of town
Who is up?
Who is down?
Where they go?
Who's to know?
But they're rolling through the snow!

Down the hills
Down the street
Never picking up their feet
Boom, bang, boink, crash
In the pond with a splash

Through the fields
Through the thickets
Get there quick, it's–
Oops...
Four speeding tickets

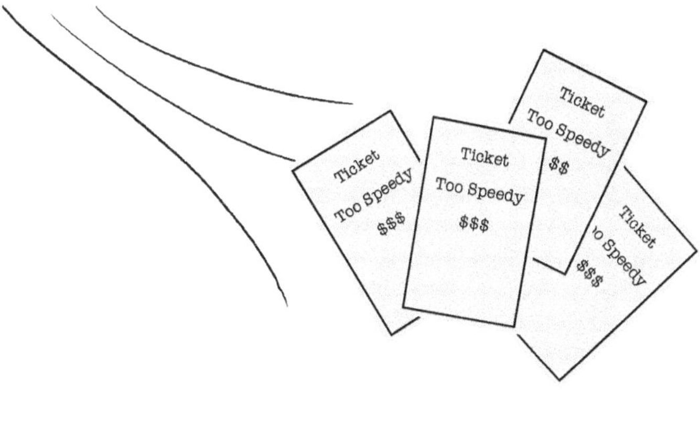

Talk about an iron pile up!

Stay Cool!

- Beatnik - One who lives like there is no tomorrow
- Blow the jets - To get angry
- Bread - Money
- Bugged - Bothered
- Blast the Edison - Turn off the lights
- Cat - Cool jazz musician
- Cool - Wonderful
- Cheap creep - Freeloader
- Can the lip - Stop talking
- Cool it - Slow down
- Crazy quilt - New dress
- To 'Cherry Tree' - To lie
- Daddy O - Term of affection
- Dig - Understand
- Fall in - To enter
- Fall out - Leave or exit
- Flick - Movie
- A groove - a thrilling thing to do
- A groovie - Someone who understands the swing of things
- A gas - Something wonderful
- Gone - Really with it, swinging
- Ginchiest - The greatest
- Germsville - Hospital
- Hep-cat - A stylish, fashionable person
- Hip - To be with it, to understand
- Hipster - Best character, musician
- Hootenanny - Wild party beat
- The Horn - Telephone

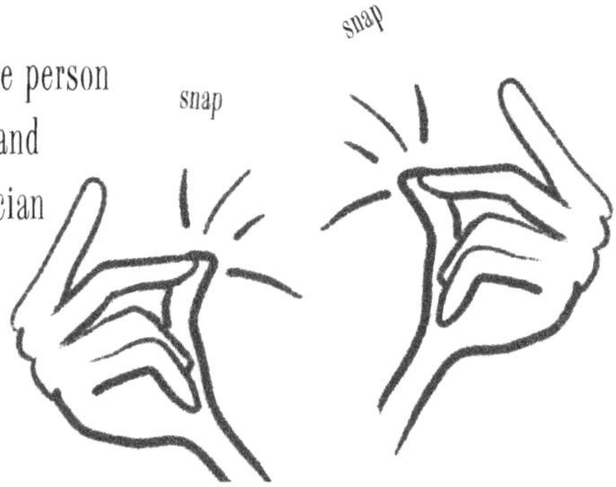

- Iron pile up - Getaway
- Kookie - Wild character
- Leathers - Shoes
- Moo juice - Milk
- Moo goo - Butter
- Moss, moss - etc. etc.
- Murgatroid - Outcast, a square
- Money run - Very easy, ordinary
- Nadaville - Nowhere, dull place
- Orbs - Eyes
- Off the wall - Very far out, extremely unusual
- Pad - Apartment
- Pick up on - To dig, to understand
- Short trip to Rio - Coffee break
- Fuzz rod - Police car
- Swinging - One who is with it
- Swinging like a sixteen - Really wild
- Shake it - Forget it
- Turn up the stereo - Listen to me
- Twin trees - High heels
- Tough toenails - Very difficult
- Tuned in - With it
- Way out - Unusual
- Wild - Terrific, unusual
- Wail - To have a good time, to play a tune well

Catch you later. It's been a real gas.

www.ingramcontent.com/pod-product-compliance
Lightning Source LLC
Chambersburg PA
CBHW040555010526
44110CB00055B/2794
9780973630879